Not Far from the River

Not Far from the River

Poems from

THE GĀTHĀ SAPTAŚATI

Translated by

DAVID RAY

Copper Canyon Press / Port Townsend

ISBN 1-55659-034-2
Library of Congress Catalog Card Number 90-81354

Some of these poems previously appeared in
Translation (Columbia University), *Poetry East,* and *Nimrod.*
A selection of these versions was published
by the Rajasthan Prākrit Bhārati Sansthan
of Jaipur, India, in 1983.

The publication of this book was supported by a
grant from the National Endowment for the Arts.

Copper Canyon Press is in residence with
Centrum at Fort Worden State Park.

Copper Canyon Press
Post Office Box 271
Port Townsend
Washington 98368

for Judy, Amrit & Prem,
Sapphina, Wesley, Wini & Sam

Introduction

One afternoon in early 1982, my wife and I were having tea with Francine and Daya Krishna in their Jaipur garden. I had been lecturing on American poetry at the University of Rajasthan, where Francine and her husband Daya were both professors. Their house was just across the road from the university; to get there, Judy and I had biked through campus between long rows of tall eucalyptus trees perfuming the air.

Francine, her sari wrapped around her, leaned forward to lift from the coffee table an unimpressive looking book with a brown grocery sack dust jacket. She had been admiring the text, *the Gāthā Saptaśati*, she said, and since the original was in Prākrit, an ancient peasant dialect of Sanskrit, the New Delhi Prākrit Society, of which she was a member, had decided to find a poet who could render the work into modern English. Would I take it along and see if I wanted the commission?

I glanced through the edition of the *Gāthās*, published by The Asiatic Society of Calcutta some years before. The text had not only the ancient Prākrit script, but also Sanskrit translations which many Indians could understand. There were also English prose versions, but they were unappealing in the extreme. The vocabulary was archaic, with frequent use of words like "horripilations," and I saw nothing poetic in these cribs. The logic was often impenetrable, forced—with only here and there the hint of a metaphysical conceit buried within the knots of language.

I took the old book along to be polite, and it bounced around in my bicycle basket as we headed back home along the dusty

7

road. I intended to return the book, but a few days later while idly browsing the text, I came across a passage that was fascinating. It embodied a curious notion—the idea of being shampooed with a lover's feet. *Kathak* dance, a style busy with footwork, had already alerted me to the fact that feet were not always so functionally atrophied as they are today.

I had become interested in *kathak* because my wife and daughter had been taking lessons from a local guru who called out the beat in Hindi for dancers whose feet pounded, leapt, and palpitated to the mesmerizing and repetitive drone of tabla, harmonium, and sarangi. Rich harmonics are built from sensual play of voice and instrument, and from the vigorous and yet subtle dances with their strong narrative of religious devotion, of myth, and of the vibrant life of villages. And with each thumping or floor-patting step, ankle bells rang out, for each dancer had looped about her foot a few heavy coils of little bells.

I began to see in the *gāthās* some of the qualities of *kathak*—a vibrant celebration of village life, of love and song and devotion. The poems, like the dance, evoke the spirit of villages some two thousand years ago, when King Hāla collected the 700 verses from a number of different poets. Furthermore, in the script of the *gāthās*, somewhat like the Hindi script we were struggling to learn, I saw strong hints of passionate flurry, of devotional involvement in the numinous phenomena of everyday life. Remnants and vestiges of a life that had once been a dance, a web of worshipful activity, seemed to have survived the ravages of history, seemed to be gleaming through, if only in fragments. Aren't Sappho and the early Greek poets known primarily through surviving fragments? I had often thought that a poem hasn't really come alive until it has suffered its sea-changes and losses through time. We never glimpse more than a partial glory from the past.

I began to play with casting the poems into idiomatic American, and to think about a form that might work. I did several in the style of the *Rubaiyat* before opting for simple and flexible unrhymed quatrains. My first rendered version of a *gāthā* was of the one that first amused and captivated me:

> *Now that I see these dancers*
> *I recall how much I enjoyed*
> *that shampoo*
> *you gave me with your feet.*

Was the amorous use of feet lost in those two thousand years, like so many customs described in these verses?

The *gāthās* reflect long-lost concerns about the etiquette and rituals of the harem as well as life in the village. I began to eliminate those verses that would require footnotes; I had no desire to explain pantheistic notions or faith that "the moon pours out ambrosia when it falls into the mouth of the god Rāhu in an eclipse." I didn't want to deal with archaic lore, e.g., certainty that throbbing in the left eye of a woman was considered auspicious for a seducer. But I found irresistible the association of love with the white lotus, peacocks as weathermen, green parrots as gossips.

Many of the poems, as I studied them more closely and enlisted friends who knew Sanskrit (and more rarely, Prākrit) to help me puzzle out the originals, illustrated that *plus ça change, plus c'est la même chose*. The passions of lovers and seekers of wisdom a full twenty centuries ago were as immediate, as recognizable as our travails and tortures, our joys and our self-deceptions.

There are several personae in the poems, inevitable because they were written by so many different poets. King Hāla, who supposedly composed forty-four of the poems himself, said that he had chosen seven hundred *gāthās* adorned with traditional metaphors out of ten million such verses. A counterpoint makes itself heard through the distinct voices, the passions balanced by reflection, one modality balanced by another. Some *gāthās* express passion, but lust has at times been left behind by those who seek transcendence. Chief characters seem to appear and reappear—the lovers, gossips, poets and philosophers. There are ladies driven mad by solitary frustration, beggars hoping to find temporary refuge, boys who hope to learn love's secrets; and that stock figure, the younger brother-in-law, his efforts at seduction tireless.

The *gāthās* present a world not found in the villages today, yet one has a sense when traveling through India that nothing has ever changed. Harem and suttee are woven into myth and collective memory. There is a sense of the gods being near, and often amused. Nature is close and familiar, each blossom with its symbolic associations, each bird with its role in the stormy passions of nature. The wanderings of the moon are meaningful, and the monsoon ominous.

The scenes these verses immortalize endure. A thousand years hence, they will still be reenacted. If there is an exchange of missiles and a nuclear winter those events may somehow be as irrelevant to the villagers as were the Dark Ages and the world wars. There is a timelessness to the life of those who are not a part of the international power struggle. In the last analysis they are all we have—the lovers—and the *gāthās* are nothing more than a celebration of those who bear the fires of Eros well.

DAVID RAY

Not Far from the River

ग्रमिश्रं पाउग्र-कव्वं पढिउं सोउं ग्र जे ण ग्राणन्ति ।
कामसूस तत्त-तन्तिं कुणन्ति ते कहँ ण लज्जन्ति ॥२॥

[1]

Why do these prudes fear Prākrit poetry,
our music, and the blunt facts of love?
They draw back from that nectar,
yet wince as if they taste love's ashes.

[2]

Out of ten million or more gāthās
King Hāla has chosen a mere seven hundred.
The reason for this is quite simple—
he preferred those that caught life in their nets.

[3]

Jewels wherever we look—
that white crane on a motionless lotus—
like a conch on a dish made of emeralds,
polished at least for a lifetime.

[4]

Rare sight, a woman lost in the trance,
making love. Beautiful—so long as her eyes
remain open, like blue of the lotus.
Then her pleasure gets ugly, too busy, intent.

[5]

She likes it, the conjugal act.
But she smiles, her lotus-like face turned,
knowing he chooses this auspicious hour of dawn
neither for her nor himself, just for good luck.

[6]

When away from their lovers
true ladies are tormented
by the budding of the wax-leaved
ashoka tree.

[7]

Chief ornament of our village,
white lotus flowers of our lake –
nothing but a heap now,
withered, ready for the fire.

[8]

If you weep already
at sight of the moon-white rice
you'll go crazy for sure
when the yellow hemp is ripe.

[9]

The way of love is crooked and fragile
like the hair on a crab or a cucumber.
Therefore you fail to impress me, weeping
with your too perfect face, round as the moon.

[10]

Mother was angry. Father fell to his knees,
kissing her feet. I climbed on his back.
She broke into laughter, dragged him away.
Years later, I figure it out.

[11]

She made a mistake in loving him.
He does not deserve the likes of her.
She should prefer death to such a dishonor.
So far, though, not one of us has told her.

[12]

A small incident, but I'll always recall it.
Mother was cooking. Father said something,
made her laugh. She touched her pale face,
smudging it black as the dark spot on the moon.

[13]

Lady so skilled in cooking,
the fire of your oven sends out smoke
to embrace you, sucks in return
your delicate breath, fragrant as the Patala.

[14]

The newly wed girl, pregnant already,
asked what she liked about the honeymoon,
cast a glance at her husband,
but not at his face.

[15]

Moon, round and white like the tilaka mark
on her face, moon on the dark face of night,
touch me, please, with the same cool hands
that have found my beloved by now, warm in her bed.

[16]

Your hairs rise up when you're kissed
and your goosebumps break out.
Quit feigning sleep
and I'll do it the way you like.

[17]

Skip the perfume
and the ointments.
He's too hot to notice.
Hurry, or it'll be too late.

[18]

She kissed me as never before,
careful not to rub foreheads
because she was smeared with that goo
village girls have to wear once a month.

[19]

She showed me how to do
everything she wanted
but in the morning
dressed behind the bamboo screen.

[20]

Doubly sorrowful, the loss of a lover
and seeing him involved with another.
Yet I honor his sense of high birth, his restraint
because he throws me not one glance of contempt.

[21]

He could never move past
a black-spotted deer, a bad omen.
But he side-steps his wife, her dark eyes
heavy with sorrow, and wet.

[22]

At dawn he leaves her half awake, one final kiss.
He whispers how he suffers to leave her.
But I'm in the worst pain of all,
reduced to zero, having watched them all night.

[23]

Both feign sleep,
listen to the breath
of the other, but one will give up,
risk an embrace.

[24]

Her husband's younger brother
knows all the tricks, touches her leg,
strokes it with that stiff cucumber vine.
Just what he wanted, bristling hairs!

[25]

Rumbling of clouds, monsoon on its way,
or drums of an execution.
I've heard both before, but seldom without
my love in my arms, enjoying our pleasures.

[26]

Too many girls in the village
are thin from wanting him.
He's cruel, afraid of his wife, elusive
and thin like a worm on a Nimba leaf.

[27]

O favored one, why should you alone
hold out? These days
there is one thing only
in the minds of all men and all women.

[28]

Why do you scorch my back
with your sighs
while I wait for a touch of your breast?
The night mocks our effort at anger.

[29]

She lives at the junction near the whores,
and her husband's away.
She's charming, youthful and ripe.
There's no moon. Yet she won't let me.

[30]

The flood trembles like a woman,
carries a great floating tree, petals
of flowers. Bees half-drowned eddy and whirl.
Some sink; others float on the current.

[31]

You'd think it would slow him,
knowing his neighbor died
in amorous sport. Still, he exerts
himself, as the entire village can hear.

[32]

It's easy to bear distance
when there's hope of reunion.
But when he's still here in the village
his absence is like death, me seeing his ghost.

[33]

His beloved comes
to his mind only now
that the arms of the slave girl
enclose him completely.

[34]

What's the use of your wretched infatuation
when not one night will ever return
for either true love or false
and youth subsides like a flood?

[35]

She knew he'd leave when dawn broke,
knew he'd return to his mistress.
So she prayed to the night, to keep him
in darkness, to hug him to death.

[36]

Because her husband is leaving
she moves from hut to hut
asking each lonesome woman
how she has managed to bear it.

[37]

She never minded his roving,
since he always wanted just one more.
That way she could hope he meant it
when he said she was best.

[38]

She let him come in,
sharing her cool room at noon,
for even a shadow seeks refuge,
and under a body's a good place.

[39]

By playing the male in this dalliance,
your hair spread like the peacock's feathers,
thighs trembling, eyes half closed,
you've learned how hard it is for us men.

[40]

Love is like water,
hot and then cold,
tepid unless it's churned up,
soon gone entirely to mist.

[41]

She could bear every sort
of dalliance without its even showing,
yet he expected her to look as limp
and withered as he was, and as forlorn.

[42]

Everyone knows she's in love,
madly seeking the man who's inflamed her.
She wanders, half delirious,
but looks right past you and me both.

[43]

A woman's a captive, caged in desire.
She mistakes the thunderbolt rumbling,
breaks out in goosebumps although
her husband's neither lightning nor thunder.

[44]

He's gone on a trip, leaving his harem.
Already they're friendly as sisters,
gossip all night,
bathe together at dawn in the river.

[45]

She kept silent about his advances,
afraid to speak to her husband.
But time's on the side of a crude lover,
even her husband's young brother.

[46]

The wise are fulfilled with inaction,
even in love,
while fools cavort to no purpose,
wrestling with love till it dies on them.

[47]

If you're not his beloved
why do you sleep half the day
and go about like a newborn calf
drunk from the first flowing milk?

[48]

She knew half of love's wisdom,
was good as they come at its skills,
but would sigh at the moon in the morning
and delay her departure like a gauche schoolgirl.

[49]

Console yourself, woman alone.
Those peaks on the mountain are lonely,
yet survive the worst season.
Spring comes, even to such peaks.

[5 0]

Offer me half, and not more.
A full draft of love I could bear,
but not the sorrow that follows,
the empty cup after.

[5 1]

He cannot be faithful and she knows it.
Therefore she wastes five days only.
On the sixth she picks out
one or two among many, eager to serve her.

[5 2]

Wherever he looks
she flicks a veil, a corner
of sari. Yet she so wants him to see
all of her, all she can offer.

[5 3]

A shrewd lover never is bothered.
Her jealousy quickly dries up.
It's a brief storm indeed,
and the aftermath is sweet.

[5 4]

A flock of green parrots
falls from the sky
like a necklace of emeralds.
But she's not looking, nor is he.

[55]

When he travels, he builds fires.
When he's in town, a brazier warms him.
But he always shivers with cold
when she's not in his arms.

[56]

Her face trembles
when she's held for a kiss,
her hair swaying, shaken,
a swarm of bees above a lotus.

[57]

All the girls of the harem are bathing.
Just one's out of step, lounging apart.
Whatever she does draws him away
from the more beautiful ones, the wet ones.

[58]

He dotes on her,
follows her about like a slave,
even saves coils of black hair
when he cleans out her comb.

[59]

Love dies if you can't get to see her
or if you see her too much,
also from the gossip of vile men.
Or from no cause at all.

[60]

A woman's love dies if she's left alone
for a month. Her lover's love dies
if he's too quickly sated. A fool's love dies
just from gossip, and a bad man's from no cause.

[61]

By the end of this season
her heart will be broken,
the tips of her breasts dark,
their full weight sad on her belly.

[62]

That fool of a wife loves him indeed.
She carries his notes to that lady,
adds her own special plea
for those full breasts to feed him.

[63]

We enjoy your visits so much,
though knowing your words are deceitful,
that we think of the pleasure
of those whom you truly adore.

[64]

Though she's turned away in her anger,
she shows him a map of desire,
for men can read goosebumps
and wise ones ignore jealous words.

[65]

Only the lady who learns
how to make love to herself
knows how to deal with that anger
that leaves her half full, half empty.

[66]

She's so shameless
that all the gossips inquire
which of her sins he'll forgive –
those past, present, or future.

[67]

There's one way to please,
be her slave.
Strangely enough it's the proud men
who truly deserve our deep pity.

[68]

You're just like a bee
who abandons one flower for another.
But all your friends agree
you have left behind the true treasure.

[69]

She went to him but was no more relieved
than one who had drunk deep
in a dream, after crawling a desert.
She always wants more.

[70]

That pitiable girl treasures his teeth-marks,
showing them off, surrounded
by goosebumps. And she has no idea
how freely he wanders.

[71]

After our lovemaking
he takes one step away to look at the moon
and returns in five minutes,
but I feel bitterly abandoned.

[72]

Pleasure and pain go together.
Even the pleasure he gives
brings its pain
since she knows he belongs to another.

[73]

No one will listen to reason
when it comes to matters of love.
They *seem* to pause, *seem* to listen,
then the madness of love gets its way.

[74]

She gathers Madhuka blossoms
weeping as if they were bones
of her husband, whom she had meant
to join on his funeral fire.

[75]

O heart, you will be burnt
by one who has burnt many – a fire of a man,
and die in a flood
by one who drowns many – a flood of a man.

[76]

Her lipstick was smeared by his kiss
as she suddenly discovers
in the bright green eyes
of her rivals, her co-wives.

[77]

When she hears of her beloved's death
she ages ten years in an hour
and sets off on her difficult path
down to the fires by the river.

[78]

I remember this pleasure –
he sat at my feet
without speaking
and my big toe toyed with his hair.

[79]

The sky has fallen,
lies heavy and blue on the lake.
But the lotus buds somehow escaped
and a few swans also survive.

[80]

Someone spoke of departure
and for that reason, I think,
that girl withers and fades
like one affected by poison.

[81]

Rare are those men
who don't grow bitter with age,
whose serenity shows in their faces,
whose kind words are passed on to their sons.

[82]

Pretending to praise their dancing
she kissed their flushed faces
and blushed deeply herself,
not your usual shepherdess.

[83]

While the Pulindas who live on the summits
crouched with bows drawn,
the pass of the mountains filled up
with billowing clouds resembling elephants.

[84]

She flirts with the bandit
and can manage a coy smile
though she is still somewhat distressed
by the murder of her husband.

[85]

Now that her husband's away
she'll use any excuse
to share, even with small boys,
that wonderful sight she sees in the pool.

[86]

That newly-wed hunter
can hardly carry his bow
and I'm sure that his arrow is limp.
In fact, he's as thin as an arrow.

[87]

The girl's such a novice at love
that she goes around saying
true lovers would die if they parted.
And she seems sincere.

[88]

Our sight of that naked woman
was a marvel, a find, and a treasure,
a kingdom in heaven, a drink from a deep glass,
yes, a nectar drunk with our eyes.

[89]

You love her while I love you,
and yet she hates you and says so.
Love ties us in knots,
keeps us in hell.

[90]

In Spring the pilgrims pause by the pines
and the breeze bears out of the forest
the humming of bees and the song
of the shepherdess, the one about her lost love.

[91]

He lives like an exile
but never will leave the village.
She's sent him far away
with her anger. So close yet so far.

[92]

Now that I see these dancers
I recall how much I enjoyed
that shampoo
you gave me with your feet.

[93]

The gods have parceled him out,
his beauty caught in my eye,
his talk in my ears, heart in my
heart, his thing in my thing.

[94]

With her eyes closed
she brought him to bed in her mind,
then did all the work with her hands
till her jingling bangles fell slack.

[95]

I'm a wretched crow
who wanders the village,
just a crumb now and then, and contempt
even from widows and hangtail dogs.

[96]

Wicked men live like the good,
enjoy a family's affection.
But they sully their walls
like defective lamps with foul smoke.

[97]

The gold of a miser
is close to him always,
but useless like the shadow
of one who wanders, starved for love.

[98]

That girl seeks you
through this village of mad dogs.
If they bite her, it'll be you,
you yourself tearing her flesh.

[99]

If the bee drinks too much,
from only the bright flowers,
it's the fault of the dry blossoms,
never the bee. He just seeks his fill.

[100]

Here ends our first hundred gāthās,
written by all the best poets,
some of them wonderful lovers,
the others mere gossips and observers.

[101]

It's really something to see, two sagging
winesacks on the open half-door.
If he doesn't come soon I'm afraid
she'll drink them herself.

[102]

I know the sight wasn't meant for me
but I saw it – those two full breasts
waiting for someone to arrive
from the town, the thirsty one.

[103]

That woman he betrayed wept
as long as she had tears to weep.
She grew thin till only the bones
were left, a dying branch creaking.

[104]

When a couple loves as they did
the one who dies first
may be said to be living
and the one remaining, truly the dead.

[105]

Girl, no need to weep.
If you place the mango blossom
over your bosom and smile
he will be unable to pass you again.

[106]

When her friends asked her why
saffron blossoms stuck to her breast
she brushed them away, only to reveal
bite marks of her lover, left and right.

[107]

When my lover is angry
even one glance of disdain
out of the corner of her eye
can truly be said to kill me.

[108]

I'll tell those ladies who refuse him
how lucky they are.
They don't heave my long sighs, weep
through the night.

[109]

O heart, give me rest,
I've served love all too well,
but now, near the end,
let me feel no attachment.

[1 1 0]

They were heavy and high in her youth
but now she must lift them herself
to admire them, to gaze
at hired teeth marks and begged-for abuse.

[1 1 1]

Never leave a deposit.
She never gives credit, permits
no withdrawal. Love left there
is wasted, gathers no interest.

[1 1 2]

She's new to it,
thinks there's still more to come,
knows well how to begin an affair,
but not how to end it, wait for another.

[1 1 3]

Let the love of harlots be sanctified.
After all, like the dalliance
of true love, it relieves
both the deep thirst and the hunger.

[1 1 4]

If you ever get what you want
your mind will never be steady.
Love's won, yet you may lose it.
You'll tremble, like all the lucky lovers.

[115]

Indeed you gave pleasure as promised,
but now you endanger my life,
simply hanging on like a weight.
Why don't you look elsewhere as well?

[116]

He forbids her to pluck the Madhuka
or even go out in the moonlight.
But he's busy himself, plucking away,
night after night, far from her side.

[117]

You seem so weary
with the weight of those breasts,
not aware of the thirst
of the young man who longs for them.

[118]

With uplifted eyes that beggar is drinking
while she pours from the jug.
But she lets it slow to a trickle
and his fingers slip apart.

[119]

The beggar stares at her navel
and her eyes can't leave his round face.
She'll give him more than the rice,
though crows fly round and grab at the bowl.

[1 2 0]

There's no choice
if you love her.
You have to make up
like a man praying to fire.

[1 2 1]

There's no one to love,
no one to tell all my thoughts.
And with whom would I share even a joke
in this wretched village of low people?

[1 2 2]

Fearing discovery by moonlight
these two sew at the leaves of the banyan,
try to stop up the chinks
that leak light.

[1 2 3]

Of course I'd like to behold her,
both her face and her hair in the breeze.
But the edge of that field near her town
is enough to delight and detain me.

[1 2 4]

Now that she's gone
he sleeps in the field, cups
the freshly turned furrow
as if it were her flank in moonlight.

[125]

Among the co-wives
who wore pearls
she walked lightly
with a single peacock feather.

[126]

Only virtue, my boy, will win over
these ladies who cast oblique glances,
who talk with allusions, walk
in sly circles, smile before you do.

[127]

O holy man, don't tempt the lion.
He has acquired the virtues
of a dog already today,
and that did not quite put him to sleep.

[128]

Clearly a god is kissing that lady,
making her nipples go stiff.
There is no way to approve of such a lover,
even if he is a god.

[129]

Your heart was so full
of the others
that you had no place for her.
Yet she loved you the most.

[1 3 0]

Although she gives me nothing but trouble,
she never leaves my heart for a moment.
And she's spoiled me for others.
I've come to treasure daily misfortune.

[1 3 1]

Awaiting him she trembles,
not knowing what she'll do when he arrives,
or what she will say. And she fears
most of all she'll have to do the work of it.

[1 3 2]

She assures him she's no longer angry,
disentangles locks of her hair
wound round his feet,
frees her anklets of silver from his hair.

[1 3 3]

From the scent of her
he knew she had bathed
in the river, with the help
of rose-apple branches.

[1 3 4]

Though she said "Go away,"
I paid more attention
to her lips, for they trembled,
and her cheeks, for they reddened.

[1 3 5]

Others leaving the boat
found the plank steady,
stepped off with no problem.
But she stumbled against him.

[1 3 6]

To this day she carries that garland
you so casually placed round her neck.
It's scentless and stale
but her eyes are still big with hope.

[1 3 7]

Though he strayed,
there was no way
she could get angry with him,
as if she'd been born without that ability.

[1 3 8]

Though her pushups look silly
please don't restrain her.
They'll prove handy
when she climbs on top.

[1 3 9]

Our village is full of young men
and she's youthful – her husband is old.
Will she die
if she says no to all lovers?

[140]

Their son's first teeth marks
on an apple, and she runs all the way
to the field where he's plowing.
She yells, but he hardly looks up.

[141]

Your own mind's the best judge.
Pay no attention to gossips.
But I'm telling you myself—
This time you've gone far too far.

[142]

No wonder my merits seem trivial
and my skills not enough for him.
She has a certain advantage, after all,
having been trained in the brothel.

[143]

He can no more see my sorrow
than a mirror sees in the dark.
Therefore I stumble in shadows
in a room he's abandoned forever.

[144]

The full summer moon equaled
the perfection of your breast,
that perfect hemisphere.
Yet it too will wane.

[145]

It's a custom to mark on the wall
a line for each day of absence.
But weeping all afternoon she's run
out of space before her first night is over.

[146]

My pleasure is greater than his,
for I treasure even one glimpse stolen
with heroic effort, and I'll never tire of her.
But he sees too much, and altogether too often.

[147]

No one else knows how
to do it that way.
One moment she gives a massage,
the next you're in heaven.

[148]

Others give wealth
and good luck,
but you have given your wives
nothing but misfortune, more than you owned.

[149]

Her face shines like the moon
and her scent is pure blossoms of apples.
But who knows what her deep kiss is like,
her hair falling over your hands?

[150]

Only the birds know for sure
where her chastity was forsaken.
They flew away from that hillside
lamenting with their *caw caw*.

[151]

Spring is the wonder of seasons,
but this time it has failed –
not even the sweet blooms of the Muravaka
will help him seduce that difficult lady.

[152]

If that errand boy only knew
how she peeked after him
like a bird in her cage,
through every slit of the fence.

[153]

If you never managed a peek
take my word for it.
First she bathes in the sun
then makes love to herself in the shade.

[154]

Afraid of putting out
the lamp
with her tears,
she moves it aside.

[155]

Don't use those half-glances.
Look with eyes open.
You'll see more,
and they'll just think that you're simple.

[156]

After a few hours of housework
she's afflicted with nerves.
One evening I calmed her.
She lay at my feet, purred like a kitten.

[157]

Your wife is more chaste than a virgin.
That is how youthful you are —
far too young to have married, unworthy
of such an opportunity.

[158]

Though the entire village burned down
we had the pleasure of seeing each other
still alive, our faces all flushed,
passing that scorched jug around.

[159]

The flood made it happen —
our meeting that will always be secret.
The moon alone was witness
to that boldness I can never repeat.

[160]

We're withered and bare
like the two trees in our yard,
and the worst part is this –
the roots of our love died years ago.

[161]

The desolate ruins of love,
sacred to the god Ananga –
hips grown old in love's service,
winesacks she must lift to her own lips.

[162]

She is so gorgeous your eyes become stuck
wherever you look – her arm, leg, belly.
No one can take in all of her beauty
because of this stickiness.

[163]

How can one woman manage it,
deadly as poison,
yet sweeter than nectar
as soon as you get close enough.

[164]

Love's absence is space through the fingers.
All trickles away. Best have the hands cupped,
sweet breast at the mouth,
not one drop spilled on the ground.

[165]

She had to claim
she'd been bitten by a scorpion
in order to see her lover,
the general practitioner.

[166]

He sold off his coat,
thinking her young breasts would warm him.
But he made a mistake.
The scorn of a woman doubles the cold.

[167]

These women plunder my husband
as if he were plums
in the bowl of a blind man.
But I can see them, clear as a cobra.

[168]

The girl was a fool,
flashing that saffron-colored scarf,
a gift from her lover,
till her husband saw it from his field.

[169]

A true expert with words
can say something that will please her,
even bring blushes to her cheeks,
yet fool that pit of snakes, the worst gossips.

[170]

There's no way I can manage a letter.
Writing your name makes me tremble
and words make everything worse.
You yourself are aware of this difficulty.

[171]

Some men never advance.
Whatever they build will fall down
and fate is watchful always
to make sure these men are never quite loved.

[172]

Angry with him, she bathed in the river
and that turmeric drifted downstream.
He waded in below her, drank deep
till his drunken antics made her adore him.

[173]

Lovers should be gentle always
because of the harsh facts:
Life is not eternal, and your love's
pale skull waits beneath her skin.

[174]

Crows eat the ripe fruit of our village,
only the crows,
because of the watchful
love-starved old gossips.

[175]

Knowing she would give in, go in the dark,
that lady began to practice
her slow and cautious steps, already
dreading both snakes and moonlight.

[176]

O moon-faced lady,
because of your big eyes
the night had twice as many hours.
And I used them all.

[177]

Sadly, the girls never learn.
A man of low birth mumbles sweet words.
But just like a dog he strolls on
when he's had what he wants.

[178]

He brought his son for the marriage,
arranged by the experts. But the bride,
turning with wide-open eyes, gave him freely
the look she should have saved for the son.

[179]

Two things bring a man down,
even from the heights of mountains –
saying he can do the work well,
or bragging when it's accomplished.

[180]

O girl at the open half-door,
whom do you seek
with hot eyes and brown nipples
that stare at the roadway?

[181]

So high they make two pillows
for her lotus-like face –
a picture of bliss on that softness.
Yet she watches the road.

[182]

The boys of our village
would know her house anywhere
from the full melons
growing on vines.

[183]

They're too much for her,
a real burden, altogether too plump,
like the double lobes on an elephant's head.
Yet men want to play there.

[184]

There's a time for it, despite what she says.
So long as it's been a month since she gave birth,
or if she's still nursing her child,
or if you catch her whenever she's laughing.

[185]

Though you might never guess it
those full, firm breasts
have been crushed against
a thousand men, maybe more.

[186]

Because of the big ones
his wife has
that peasant enjoys greatly
all the holidays.

[187]

Because of his absence
that marigold girl sat
by her doorway, withered
like a garland of welcome.

[188]

Near the old banyan the travelers paused,
clapped hands, laughed with delight
when a dozen green parrots flew out
like young leaves in a storm.

[189]

I laughed when I saw it.
He fell to kissing her feet
and she drew the lamp near
as if to examine his foolishness.

[190]

Sometimes there's a tax on virtue,
at least in this life.
One gives way, using the strength
from the past life, hope from the next.

[191]

If he's admired by the village
even his contempt is found charming.
But if he has no standing among men
even a low girl is ashamed of his love.

[192]

Her ripe breasts have fallen,
a burden now, and a bother.
Even so, no man hangs long
on the stem of her love.

[193]

He knew what she loved,
neither himself nor another.
He shared the wine
but she got the joy of it.

[194]

After one glimpse of her
he surrendered himself,
was a fool ever after, a bull in mire.
Nor was he the first she dragged down.

[195]

Friendship with a bad man —
a line drawn on water;
with a good man — etched forever,
deep script in white marble.

[196]

O doer of a daring deed indeed,
I regret you can't stay,
at least till my hair's in its braid again
and my toes can uncurl.

[197]

In town he studied seduction.
Now he lures us one by one to his hut.
But none of his tricks can arouse,
leave us aglow like unplanned encounters.

[198]

I don't know how we escaped.
We were tied in the strongest of nets,
and his arms made a tight cage around me.
Yet somehow, even my two breasts are free now.

[199]

Her beauty cannot be contained.
Those drops of dew on her belly,
trickling in and out of her navel,
are gifts to the earth, coins to the hungry.

[200]

One jasmine, the Navamālikā,
smells like a sweet vagina.
It allures us in moonlight,
gives its scent freely.

[201]

In the wayside inn the maid lay awake,
not happy until
she could hear the bangles of her mistress
jingling as that lady thrashed on her bed.

[202]

The mind of a wise man
remains constant even in adversity,
like straight rays of the sun,
golden through dusk.

[203]

Birds and men both
fill their bellies
with no concern for the poor and distressed.
But the best rescue others.

[204]

Antelope and their mates know
all about marriage,
how to make beds on straw or on snow,
how to roam forests together, love until death.

[205]

Even in summer's worst
the best way to cool off—
far better than massage or a swim—
is mutual embrace, in any position.

[206]

Aware of their poverty
the young woman hid her desire for a child,
said never a word,
climbed on top to make love.

[207]

Down the streets of our village
she runs, chasing her boychild
who's afraid of his first haircut.
And her long braids fly out behind her.

[208]

Strange how this man has survived,
as if wrinkles and grey hair were attractive.
He's lost the nubile young girls,
but the high-born ladies welcome him as ever.

[209]

All the whores chase this boy,
the only chaste male in our village.
One by one they've got hold of him,
like cupping water in their hands.

[2 1 0]

The leaves of our banyan,
sere and dry now, fall one by one.
Women also descend,
despite their great beauty, shaken by wind.

[2 1 1]

She can't seem to focus her eyes
and her sighs are heavy.
She speaks with half words.
There's got to be a reason.

[2 1 2]

Surprised with her new lover,
the housewife is quick to explain.
"This man needs a bed for the night.
He offered to pay, if he could try it."

[2 1 3]

Her hair is heavy from bathing,
perfumed, still dropping blossoms.
She lets it fall on his chest
so that he laughs and rallies again.

[2 1 4]

She was always a quick thinker.
But this time she surpassed herself.
"He came all this way to see you," she said,
shoving her lover toward her husband.

[215]

Most of the women of the world
are beautiful on one side only.
But she alone is perfect
both on the right and the left.

[216]

I dance as he plays on his flute.
A creeper wraps wavering vines
round a tree with deep roots.
My love will never be steady like that.

[217]

Though he was faithful as a slave
I falsely accused him.
Only then he started to stray
and now there's no bringing him back.

[218]

She used up her fingers and toes,
counting the days of his absence,
decided to count her two breasts,
two buttocks, each hair, before giving up.

[219]

Her love-apples are withered like winesacks.
Her eyes glow out of black hollows.
Yet, painting her face,
she feels the old jealousy, burns with it.

[220]

Leaving aside her pearls
she wore only the necklace of berries.
He found them delicious,
bent to suckle them.

[221]

Her back bears the prints
of strewn leaves.
All the gossips look at his knees,
seeking the matching design.

[222]

With her hands
she can cover her eyes.
But how can she cover her body,
goosepimpled all over?

[223]

The lightning reveals a scene
that darkness had hidden in kindness,
that woman sitting in sorrow,
weeping for her straw house swept away.

[224]

In this huge nest of gossips
there's no salt for good meat, no fire.
And it spoils in the kitchen, longing
for salt, for oil, and for fire.

[225]

She's not given up hope.
She failed to find it –
that bare spot you mentioned – in the canes.
But she has another in mind.

[226]

A good man kills pride
like a tiger.
And needs no wealth, either.
He kills that tiger as well.

[227]

Quarrels leave debris in the mind.
Words said in anger linger for years,
rotten straw, along with foul secrets.
But all get consumed on the fire.

[228]

Who would dare look in her eyes,
bright as blue lotuses
till sharp pleasure closes them,
after they've trapped what they wanted.

[229]

He worked all day, his plow
deep in the mire.
That night his wife lay restless,
her eyes wide open, counting each raindrop.

[2 3 0]

Love's a medley of terrors,
jealousy, unrelieved passion,
terrible conduct, lies, hell of parting.
Worst of all, it's not fatal.

[2 3 1]

How cruel can you get,
refusing her? She must still carry
those sweets about,
looking for a man with more gratitude.

[2 3 2]

Somehow it gave them more pleasure
in the dark, with the lamp out –
their breath half-suppressed, lips
bitten, whispering.

[2 3 3]

Because her husband was away
and the house had no lock
she asked her neighbor to join her,
to prevent burglaries and loneliness.

[2 3 4]

How long must I think of you,
like a priest staring into space,
before that wavering image
becomes your face, then the rest of you.

[235]

Lady, your great fading beauty
is like a country returned to –
impressive ruins,
your eyes two pools gone stagnant.

[236]

Their eyes exchanged message enough
and they both felt themselves lovers.
But they never got a chance
and their longing burned through the nights.

[237]

If, as you say,
you don't love him,
why do your eyes open and close
like lotuses, at mention of his name?

[238]

Your husband laughed at the fool
who offered you flowers, stupidly saying
your face was lovely like the full moon.
But later the poor cuckold repented of his folly.

[239]

The glances of that woman
would undo any man,
even one who truly loves his wife,
or a priest long devoted to the gods.

[240]

While life remained in my limbs
I bore, somehow, the burden of love.
But now I can be said to be dead
I endure days in a numbness, attached to no one.

[241]

Ladies should never speak of love
or the ways of their lovers.
For the whores always hear
and steal away the good ones.

[242]

He blushed
and his new bride laughed and embraced him,
for the knot he had meant to undo
was already untied.

[243]

She weeps, yet trembles with joy.
Her arms wrap around him
just like vines of the creeper
with lives of their own, hardly hers.

[244]

Boys plucking flowers for *puja*
should avoid the banks of the river.
The gods have no use at all
for blossoms crushed on a lovebed.

[245]

He stood at her door,
hoping to do more than sell melons
but he had not the skill
of the one who brought coconuts.

[246]

She lay so complaisant,
so exhausted from love
that that fool of a plowman
ran back to his field, thinking she was dead.

[247]

A sage asked the king:
What else on this earth
is soft as billowing clouds,
makes a sky of your chest?

[248]

She waits in the reeds,
ready for love, her gown already undone.
But hearing the withered leaves crushed,
fears this time will be her last.

[249]

She pretended to sleep, but turned over.
How could I go on being angry,
hold back from her love,
when her breast like a blossom touched my face?

[250]

The boy has been told
by her glances and half-glances.
But somebody will have to tell him
how to read such signs.

[251]

Having chanced to glimpse two lovers,
the plowman's son goes back to that spot,
gazes sadly upon it
as if he'll never enjoy such a sport himself.

[252]

He was far too carried away with her,
his mind stuffed full of her virtues.
He let her commit every kind of offense
so long as she returned by midnight.

[253]

That poor girl is weeping
because she remembers her lover.
It's a full flood of grief,
yet joy fights for life in its currents.

[254]

Since her lover's been gone
she's found a way to replace him.
She walks the same way he does
and casts glances in a male manner.

[255]

She sweeps up that straw
in the morning, wishing
she had not bent toward the floor
to prepare a bed for that guest.

[256]

Good men can never be lovers,
for they must keep themselves constant,
tell the truth most of the time,
keep the tigers of passions in cages.

[257]

Wife number one heaves a sigh,
heavy indeed,
when she sees the breast heave
on his favorite these days, the young one.

[258]

Even an elephant feels it,
grief for the love who has gone.
He holds in his trunk the sweet lotus,
lets it wither, looks so sad.

[259]

Thinking her lover was coming
she felt midnight arrive in two minutes.
But dawn took a full year to arrive
while she wept, lamenting his betrayal.

[260]

She's bewildered, knows not her own heart.
So you have to grab hold of her
while she's out gazing at stars,
something she's done nightly for weeks.

[261]

Strange that the bee makes a choice,
for not one lotus would fail him.
Each has that nectar, that fragrance.
Yet he wanders, just sampling.

[262]

Lakshmi, a goddess, was born from the sea.
Gods saw her glistening with foam.
And the travelers all halt, stare unblinking
at the plowman's daughter, wet from the river.

[263]

Peacocks dance to one music,
that of the thunder.
Smelling the rain they stretch out
their necks, long for the great monsoon.

[264]

The breast of that noble lady
is full as the moon
peeping out from between blue clouds
and it, too, promises madness.

[265]

They say a lady is fortunate
if she sees her lover in dreams,
but I get no sleep without him
and I fear another gets him in dreams.

[266]

The traveler is warmed by the sun,
also by glimpses of women.
But he cools himself off,
his face near a lotus.

[267]

There's no scorn like a lady's
and he'll never know why,
whether he asked her too late or too early
or suggested the wrong place.

[268]

These poems about love
are as sweet as ambrosia,
charming by nature, filled to the brim
with lovers and lovemaking, nectar and poison.

[269]

O heart, burn if you must,
be boiled if you choose to.
Or burst if you can't help it.
But I've left him because he's so faithless.

[270]

The wax-leaved ashoka tree bursts into bloom
if a beautiful woman kisses it.
But she stands shy,
afraid to be tested.

[271]

She so longed to join her husband,
burning with ghee on his ghat,
that she put out the fire with drops
off her face and fainted away.

[272]

I just happened to notice,
one nipple hard as a cherry,
her other limp as a goat's,
lover on one side, husband on the other.

[273]

She'll remember him always,
not just his tongue and his cock,
but the way he looked back at her limbs
when dalliance had come to an end.

[274]

None of the old ones had seen this,
the lake's bottom. But now
at the end of dry autumn, we stroll
among turtles, think how high waters served.

[275]

A girl longing for dalliance
should never set out in the dark.
The flame of desire burns bright,
far too bright in the dark.

[276]

A fire broke out by the river,
burned all the reeds.
All the gossips know why
with scorched brows she's distracted.

[277]

Only those women are happy
who have never laid eyes on this man.
They alone can sleep, hear what others say,
and not speak in faltering words.

[278]

Not what you meant
when you gave her too much.
Now she walks with a sway
though she used to be shy, delicate, faithful.

[279]

He's caught in the crossfire –
my scorn when he goes to you,
your fury when he's back with me.
And yet we are sisters, or should be.

[280]

The moon brings delight to all eyes.
Few get their fill of just looking.
She too makes men look like fools,
their eyes always wide open, staring.

[281]

In our day blue bees made such a weight
on those bowers of cane
that they bent over the river and broke.
Now they are withered, no shelter for love.

[282]

Her love was an image in dreams.
She gave me anything I desired.
But when I woke and looked for her
she had gone, just like a dream.

[283]

The bow's limber yet serves
the arrow so straight.
Can it ever be constant, this tension,
held for a savoring moment?

[284]

All who noticed expressed wonder.
She seemed no more than a girl.
But the touch of that first lover
gave her the breasts of a goddess.

[285]

They wear bronze medals with pride
because they performed well in battle.
You could say they were heroic,
marked from a recent skirmish.

[286]

Who does not like it, the touch
of breasts plump, no space between,
just as one loves Prākrit poems
devoid of fault, rich with figures of speech?

[287]

Only when she is sure
of this embrace
does she fling aside
that dangling necklace.

[288]

Men and women of bronze bear the fire
of Eros well, let it burn hot as hell.
Then there are those others –
consumed like paper with the first flame.

[289]

The clouds are grunting with effort
hoping to pull the earth up
on those millions of strings
strong as the best hammered silver.

[290]

He broke her bracelets in love-play
but she was foolish indeed to accuse him
in front of his wife –
that wretched, simple-minded girl.

[291]

Her beauty's so great
her earrings seem to drink it.
Her cheeks have a goldenish nectar
that spills into those small silver cups.

[292]

She meant to send a messenger
with her note and a flower,
but before she knew it
she found herself at his gate, wet with dew.

[293]

I return through the mud
but on my way to you
did not even notice
such wetness, such sliminess.

[294]

When the lady's on top
her hair's a splended curtain, swaying.
Her earrings dangle, her necklace shakes.
And she's busy, a bee on a lotus-stalk.

[295]

O Krishna, you wander in our village,
make love with all manner of girls.
Only in this way, so you tell us, can a man
learn the difference between good, better, best.

[296]

How familiar the words.
But just once in a lifetime
a woman hears a man praise her
because unselfish love wells up in his heart.

[297]

She listened and smiled
till his words became sharp with desire.
That's when she sent him away,
wishing lust had not ruined him.

[298]

When they stopped
she was embarrassed by her nakedness
but since she couldn't reach her clothes
she pulled him upon her once more.

[299]

Even an old cow
gives fresh milk
at an expert touch,
will moo with gratitude.

[3 0 0]

He stands silent and stunned,
having chanced to glimpse
those women at the river,
rising with thin clothes clinging.

[3 0 1]

Though guided only by instinct
her skills were amazing.
He accused her of being trained
in a brothel.

[3 0 2]

She's so sad at being pregnant again,
and for one reason only –
that she has no taste for climbing
on top, or other things he desires.

[3 0 3]

You tell me we should see each other
though our love has cooled. But when,
please tell me, has a heart been helped
by being split open again?

[3 0 4]

As she was alone, altogether abandoned,
it must have seemed perfectly appropriate
that the moon was round, pale
and empty – the lake waters wide and inviting.

[305]

You never thought you'd warm to her,
wife of your worst enemy. But she asked you
to reach a ripe mango, high in the tree,
and looked up with that giveaway smile.

[306]

At the carnival
he made just one mistake,
calling out the name of his Beloved
to his Beloved.

[307]

For a time they were truly in love.
Their desire was fulfilled, and they trembled.
For six months at least they could not believe
other men and women lived on this earth.

[308]

Because of those nit-picking gossips,
wretched people making mountains
out of molehills, I cannot even look
at her out of both eyes at once.

[309]

If you can't bring him to his knees
with that glance like an arrow
and that musical walk you've perfected
he's a *sanyasi*, a holy man for sure.

74

[3 1 0]

The bride's mother looked away,
having nothing to distract her.
She had noticed the groom's teethmarks
revealed by the wind and the fluttering sari.

[3 1 1]

Young men are so bitter about love
they won't calm down, regard us as friends.
Believe it or not, each of these tea-drinking
old men once sipped at the poison of lust.

[3 1 2]

The creepers grow over her doorway,
blocking the gaze of those passing by.
A great loss, since many a traveller
has found relief through that half-open gate.

[3 1 3]

She's wasting away
yet is ripe as juicy berries.
What a crime that nobody crushes
that softness to his lips.

[3 1 4]

Which would you have, sweetness
of sugar cane or that man's honeyed words?
Both cause bliss in the mind, blushes and goosebumps,
and make a girl want to be loved.

[3 1 5]

That fortunate lamp and the mirror
are witness to all their fine loveplay.
So the lamp will never go out
and the mirror will always be watching.

[3 1 6]

Take that damned parrot away.
He repeats all our love talk
to everyone in the village,
has them gathered around him.

[3 1 7]

Eyes dilated, goosebumps on breasts,
those ladies wading in deep
reveal no other response
to their secret lovers, swimming like fish.

[3 1 8]

It's a picture, but not such a pretty one.
The green parrots fly out of a tree.
They look just like the flung vomit
disgorged by a craggy-faced drunk.

[3 1 9]

It's the first time he's left her.
Two days now, he's already in tears
at sight of the fragrant, ripe flower.
But in time he will travel, and often, by choice.

[320]

A trusting husband, foolish old farmer.
He looks to the sky, doubting the moon.
But it doesn't occur to him to notice
those half-moon marks on his faithless wife.

[321]

How much can one say with words
or convey in the code of a letter?
You yourself are aware of this problem
and of the sorrow and silence I suffer.

[322]

Whose hands, I can't help but wonder,
will rest on those fabulous breasts,
glistening like true treasure jars,
good for tipping up, for deep drinking.

[323]

Her husband is strong as an ox
but he can't keep the men
from sneaking looks at her.
She's got the best ones in the world.

[324]

It's not the best river, perhaps.
Others have green banks, musical waters,
antelope near, look lovely.
But for love under water, ours is the best.

[325]

Come and look at these two,
high and without peer, plump
on her chest,
ripe bilva fruits meant for the lucky.

[326]

How long will I enjoy her embraces?
I know she's a vagrant of love,
moving here and there, wherever
a hungry glance takes her, as mine did

[327]

You're so used to illicit love, jumping up
when the cock crows, that you can't even
wake up at home without instinctive alarm,
the furtive embrace, rushing out.

[328]

The parrot gave us away,
gossip and teller of tales.
When I warned you, you just laughed
and refused to cover his cage.

[329]

When the bee becomes greedy
there is no action he withholds.
He makes love to those buds and wet petals.
You'd think he had studied our love poems.

[3 3 0]

He's not even interested
in flowers
but asks her to lift again and again
still another garland, tell him the price.

[3 3 1]

Ungrateful, forgetful,
your mind free of the bower of reeds
that kept out the sun –
and you forgot the river as well.

[3 3 2]

We should love like those deer.
Even the hunter with his arrow drawn
had to set aside his bow, weep
for the tender glance of each for each.

[3 3 3]

He says she's a whore, uses rough words
to describe what he's seen through the reeds.
But if she did it with him
he'd speak of her sweetly – same woman, same tricks.

[3 3 4]

Girl with your sari in wind,
cover your hips or they'll laugh.
Two beggars are pointing already
at those half-moons of teeth-marks.

[3 3 5]

Let those who want sainthood
keep to their path of denial – no harm.
But I know what I want, and wait
for a chance for my eyes to say so.

[3 3 6]

The love gods have special affection
for women who like it on top,
their hair fanned out, disheveled,
eyes closed, their thighs trembling.

[3 3 7]

She showed him a sample,
letting her blue bodice fall open
though he was the one
come to sell melons.

[3 3 8]

In autumn the dusty travelers
bend to the lake,
sip near the fragrant blue lotuses
as if kissing the faces of their wives.

[3 3 9]

They found each other at the same moment,
both with their eyes half afire.
So that no one could have said
which looked first, or was hungrier.

[340]

Pray for the summer,
the beds made of reeds, places of secret,
perfume and shelter of tall flowers,
rank-smelling, intoxicating.

[341]

If it's deerskin you want
you're asking the wrong hunter.
I don't bend my bow against deer,
having seen them, like me and my love.

[342]

She was ready to follow,
into the fire of cremation, in suttee.
But because of her readiness, her hot love,
he came back to his life, joined her anew.

[343]

It is the fortunate who live
in the mountains
where bamboo always hides lovers
and music of brooks babbles on.

[344]

The cow that would give nothing at all
now offers a river of milk.
The good herdsman must do more
than gaze longingly at her.

[345]

He's so lonesome
he touches the leaf with soft down,
rubs it all over his body
as if it were her soft cheek or her breast.

[346]

Bride and groom have been blessed
and it's time to pull her away.
But she shyly holds back
to hear the songs of her sisters.

[347]

The new bride's regarded as treasure,
yet she will not even look at him
nor allow herself to be touched
or say anything at all. She just trembles.

[348]

Hearing his name, you get goosebumps.
His words calm you, just like a massage,
and I notice you tremble when you glimpse him.
I expect an explosion when you embrace.

[349]

The woman has so trained her dog
that he welcomes her lover
but growls at her husband, bares his teeth
when that poor man returns from the field.

[3 5 0]

O clever and affectionate poverty,
how you love to cling to those
who are accomplished, liberal,
possessed of subtle, unbearable knowledge.

[3 5 1]

She dares you to look at the moon
and keep looking
as she lets her robe fall open.
And you don't know what's so funny!

[3 5 2]

The buffalos are led away
by the butchers, swords raised up high,
and they look back with big black eyes
saying farewell to the village.

[3 5 3]

If you don't wipe your tears
your lover will think
your face is wet always,
never dry for a kiss.

[3 5 4]

That man's so accustomed to illicit love
that even when he's at home
he leaps up when the cock crows
and takes flight through the mud.

[355]

Even a god, when he mutters a mantra,
stumbles if he sees reflected
such a lotus-like face. Salute him,
but shun his bad habits. Pray with eyes closed.

[356]

Our Prākrit poems end here, compiled
by King Hāla. Who could refuse to be moved
by their charm, or wish sincerely
we had held our tongues, speaking of love?

About the Translator

David Ray spent 1981–82 in India on an Indo-U.S. Fellowship. In addition to his versions of the Prākrit, he recently published a volume of poems, *The Maharani's New Wall* (Wesleyan University Press), which also draws on his experience in India. He is the author of many books of poetry, including *Sam's Book* and *Gathering Firewood: New Poems and Selected*. He has won the 1989 Nebraska Review Poetry Award, the 1988 Maurice English Poetry Award, the William Carlos Williams Award from the Poetry Society of America for *The Tramp's Cup*, a National Endowment of the Arts fellowship for fiction, and several PEN/NEA Syndicated Fiction awards for short stories. Since 1971, he has been a professor at the University of Missouri-Kansas City.

Cover photo is of Krishna playing flute from an Indian temple.
The type is Kennerley, designed by F.W. Goudy.
Composition by The Typeworks, Vancouver, B.C.
Book design by Tree Swenson.
Book Manufactured by McNaughton & Gunn.